All Rights Reserved

Miami, Florida
purposedriveninitiatives@yahoo.com
www.pdi-publishing.com
www.purposedriveninitiatives.com

Book Layout © 2015 PDI Publishing
Front Cover Artwork: Cristina Acosta Art & Design LLC
Book Layout Design: Iandesigns
Printed in the USA
Through My Eyes/Janine Hernandez-1st Ed.
ISBN 978-0-692-46812-8

Through My Eyes

By Janine Hernandez

Through My Eyes

Table of Contents

Poetry has always been a way for me to escape the realities of life and enter into a world of great imagination. Through the hardest of times, journaling and poetry have been my backbone to succeed and get ahead. ***Through My Eyes*** is a compilation of my thoughts, poetry and inspirations. Enjoy.

Tea Time…

My name is Janine Hernandez. I am a mother, a daughter, a sister, and a friend… I am an ambitious woman with aspirations to change the world one person at a time. I am a leader, and a mentor. I affirm myself to be independent, intelligent and free. I cultivate happiness and my sole purpose in life is to fulfill the vision God has for me.

Poetry has always been a great part of me. This book represents my poetry work from my teenage years.

This book is dedicated to my son Jamil Angel Bautista, for he constantly pushes me into my purpose and is the catalyst that motivates me.

Thank you to my family for the support they have shown throughout the years.
A special thank you to my editor Jessica Restrepo, to my mentor Vasti Amaro for constantly providing the knowledge and guidance to properly execute my goals and vision; to Celeste Duckworth for always believing in my work and inspiring me to publish my book. Thank you to Y. Nelson Thomas, I remember when you helped me create my "Life's Mission Statement" and affirmations. It is something I still use to this day!
www.pdi-publishing.com

Love Caused Scents is a poem that I wrote when I was sixteen! Till this day, I am still surprised at the talent I had at that age. It is one of those poems that can have several different meanings; it just depends on how the reader would like to interpret it. When I wrote the poem I envisioned the "aroma" to be the guy's personality. And the "cologne" to be the scent the guy chose to be. I wanted to express my feelings in a confusing way, if that makes sense. *Love Caused Scents* is one of my favorite poems because when you are sixteen you dream of growing up and getting married, and finding the perfect guy.

Love Caused Scents

The sweet scented aroma of the cologne you chose
Attracted me to you as if you were that one single wet rose
That one single wet rose I had been waiting for my whole life
You bent on one knee and said "will you wed to be my wife"
Good days and bad days we will go through it together
The cologne you chose is what made us a forever
Maybe there is something more than just that sweet scent
But I know you were the one when I got the message God sent
One single wet rose is what I have found
Now it's not so single, because that aroma made us one
ground.

I vividly remember when I wrote *"Poetry"*. When I was done I thought to myself, "Wow, this is amazing!" It is a reflection of how I truly felt at that point in time. I felt like no one in the world understood me but my poetry. I felt like poetry was my only friend, the only thing that was there to listen to my sadness, my happiness, and my thoughts. Poetry is my only true friend.

<u>Poetry</u>

I take out my paper and write
I tell you what I have in sight
I never thought I could feel like this
But poetry's within my rights
I jot down my feelings and soul
I tell you what I feel and more
Emotions seem to take a toll
But poetry's what I adore
The times that I have been sad
And times that I've gotten real mad
The only thing that was there for me was
Poetry

Poetry My Only Friend

9 O'clock Love is one of those poems that you write when you are thinking about marriage as a little girl. You dream of one day finding that one guy that will sweep you off your feet. That was this poem. Just what every girl dreams of.

9 O'clock Love

It was 8:59 when you walked through the door
9:00 stared in your eyes and I knew you'd change my world
You were dressed real casual in your nice blue tie
My heart melted and I felt as if I could fly
The scent of your cologne sent shivers through my body
At that very moment I knew you'd be that special somebody
You handed me a rose still fragrant and wet
It symbolized our love since the moment we met
You touched my hand so gentle and soft
As you bent on one knee and started to talk
I cried with emotions because I knew what would come
That one simple question that would make us one
You looked in my eyes and dug in your soul
As you said, "Will you be my wife forever and to hold?

Ladies, do you ever feel like you wish you knew what your guy what thinking about or feeling? Men will say things, or act a certain way, but they are completely different from women. I wrote *Mysterious Man* because I wish I knew what goes on in their mind and heart. What do they think about? Why are they mysterious? Why do they act a certain way? Do they cry when no one is around? Do they really regret things they do or say? I guess you will never really know with a mysterious man.

Mysterious Man

He walks around with this gleam in his eyes
This mysterious man caught my attention
There's something about him I'm not going to lie
As if I've known him forever, I'll mention
He's the only one who gives me emotional affection
And never gets mad if I ask dumb questions
I'm glad we have that mysterious connection
Because after all we've been through it takes a lot of
dedication

The One

Through all the sorrow that has been caused
Never thought I would stop to think and pause
That you would be the one to cherish me
And take me to that place where I want to be
You never think you learn to love
The one who guides you from above
The one who frees you from all your deliverance
Yet makes you smile though all the distance.

My Sunny Day

You are like the sun in the sky
Shining down on me
You're like the air I need to breath
You know I can't deny
How I feel inside
That you and I were destined to be

Short, Sweet, and to the point. When you are in love nothing else matters!

I'll Be

When you have tears of sadness falling down your cheeks
I'll be the one to dry them and you won't feel so weak
When you feel low deep down inside and you don't have
much pride
I'll be the one there because you know you can confide
When you don't feel too good and you feel insecure
Know that pain that you have I will take and endure

My Guardian Angel is made for that someone special that you feel is always looking out for you, taking care of you, and making sure you feel right. A wonderful blessing, a wonderful friendship, something that will never end. Guardian angels are there forever, until the end of time.

My Guardian Angel

Out of all the many blessing in my life
God chose you to be my light
To guide me and show me the way to heaven
I couldn't have asked for a better present
My angel, my love, my very best friend
You've watched over me since the beginning and will till the
end
So I say to you now with oh so much love
Thank you my angel, my heavenly dove.

I Appreciate

I appreciate the way you make me feel
Knowing that everything you say is real
I appreciate the way you set everything aside
Just to make sure that I am feeling alright
I appreciate all the great moments we share
Even though I don't see you that often it only seems fair
I appreciate the times you make me smile
By saying "have a good day, make it worth your while"
I appreciate the times I need someone to talk to
You're always there to help me see what's true
I appreciate this friendship and bond that we have
Now I have learned how blessed I am

Calls that Count

You call me up its 12:46
I want to let you know that's a call I won't miss
You laugh it off cause you know I was sleeping
But don't hang up cause you're the one who id been dreaming
You tell me how you've been and that you're okay
While all I am thinking in my head is if you'll come my way
I tell you I miss your talk and you tell me you miss mine too
You tell me to be waiting for you because March is coming soon

March is the month that you want to come
The month you've left open so we can have some fun
It's been 8 minutes into our conversation and you say you have to go
You say you have a meeting tomorrow and that's something I should know

You tell me to be careful be safe and be good
As I listen to your voice I get in a good mood
I interrupt you to say thank you for the call
Calls like these make me jump off the wall
You reply me a your welcome and for you it's the same
Tomorrow you'll phone me because it will be another day
I say I love you with all of my heart
I'm surprised to hear and I love you too before the phone clicked with a spark.

All of Me

I want to rest my head against your chest
To feel your heartbeat as it works at its best
To hear it thump to hear it sway
Makes me feel as if we are one on that day
To have my hands compressed against yours
Makes me feel safe as if I'm taking a special tour
Your brown complexed skin is so soft and smooth
For it feels so enticing… yes I'm telling the truth
Being with you, makes me cry with emotions
Cause I feel for you strongly and its more than a love potion
Every second spent with you is a blessing made in heaven
Not only do you care for me but you make me feel worth living
Baby I'm so glad you're of the male gender
You may be manly and masculine but you treat me with much tender
I'm ready to give you all of me
Even if it means I'm going to loose my virginity
Cause you deserve nothing but the best
Now let's take everything and put it to our test

It Doesn't Matter

No matter what you say
I'm always going to be this way
No matter what you think
I'm never going to change
Because I am who I am
I won't subside doing what I do
I won't falter in my dreams
Because I still believe
I am much stronger now
And I'm not feeling down
Cause through it all
I will always stand tall

34

Moments in Life

No matter how many times we argue
No matter how many time we disagree
Remember that I still love you
And together we'll always be
Through the good times in our life
And the bad ones we try to erase
If we stick together always
Then there's nothing we can't face

Sweet kisses, sweet hugs is one of those fun poems you write when you're just in love and being silly. You sometimes act silly when you are in love.

Sweet Kisses, Sweet Hugs

Sweet kisses, sweet hugs that's something I would love
Sweet kisses, sweet hugs from a heavenly dove
A tender touch from a tender hand
A love dream captured from this wonderful man
Nights of passion days of delight
Sweet kisses, sweet hugs will take us on that flight
A sparkle of light will reflect on my face
This true love will never erase
Tinkles of raindrops will fall on my body
Sweet kisses, sweet hugs from that special somebody

I didn't write ***"Can I walk with you"*** for anyone in particular but I know there comes a point in everyone's relationships where you realize you want to take the relationship further. And maybe it's not necessarily by getting married just yet however; you want to express how you feel at that specific moment. This poem is allowing all lovebirds out there to let their significant other know that they want to spend more time together, do more things, see more places, learn and grow together but without directly implying marriage or engagements.

Can I Walk with You?

I want to walk with you as I hold your hand tight
Walking with you through life as I hold on with all my might
Our hands touching as we stroll through our paths
Never letting go is what will make it last
We'll overcome any bumps on the way there
But when we reach our destination well know it was fair
Walking with you would be one wish
I can tell this from the moment we kissed
You're unique and different from everyone else
This is something I have always felt
I want to walk with you through life as I hold on to you tight
Never letting go, hoping someday you'll be mine
"Will you walk with me?"

I know women cry, and sometimes a lot. We don't contain our emotions as well as men do. I wrote this poem thinking about how men bring out their emotions. When they eventually have bottled everything up and can't take it anymore they tend to break down. Some out of anger, some out of sadness, some out of depression etc. I was thinking about how they too may have a dreadful soul at hard times in their life, whether it's a breakup, a death in the family, or a failure in their life that they just beat themselves over for it. In this poem I wanted to make sure I was that girl that dries up those tears and patches up those wounds…

Dreadful Soul

I must find out what dreads him bad
Though he might deny, it I'll find out fast
The tears fall down his smooth soft face
I must comfort and sooth him with my embrace
To see him happy with that sweet smile
Fills me with joy every once in a while
To see him dread, tears my heart into pieces
For this man is my soul mate and he completes my wishes
Agony and pain is what he feels
Through it all I'm by his side to make him feel what's real

My mother, at one time, operated the city buses. I remember I behaved badly one day, maybe by talking back to her or something, I don't quite remember. My punishment was to ride the city bus all day. I remember sitting there and the only possible option I had was to observe what the other people were doing, who walks in, where they are heading to, listen to conversations. I tried to come up with all sorts of ideas to keep myself entertained and not get bored. I thought of this poem and texted myself on my cell phone so I wouldn't forget.

Bus

They get on this same bus every day
Each person is different in many ways
What is it that joins them all together?
Is it maybe all the outside bad weather?
Whatever it may be they will always be joined
Together as one for a minute
On this dirty bus coined

"Fire that grew" is about being confused in a relationship but reassuring yourself that everything is perfectly fine because ultimately the friendship or fire grew so it doesn't matter what you are thinking or what you are going through... Your together and happy.

Fire that Grew

I hate the way you aren't here
I hate the way I fear
I hate the way I feel you'll leave
Yet I love the way you're still here
I wish I could tell you how I feel
Though it's pointless cause you already know
I wish I could tell you I love you my dear
Cause you seem to make me glow
I may hate things I may love things,
I may suffer because you're not near
But deep down inside I know it's not a lie
That's why I cry happy tears
Our friendship caught fire and the sparks grow every day
That's the reason why I wish you will stay
I hate the way I'm impatient
Yet I love the way I'm patient
Cause one day I know that fire will grow... And grow
I may hate things, I may love things
I may suffer because you're not near
But deep down inside I know it's not a lie
That's why I cry happy tears

Perfect Night

Your sexy voice is so soothing to me
With you is exactly where I want to be
In your arms cuddled under the stars
Just the two of us, doesn't matter where we are
With passion I want to kiss your soft lips
As our bodies touch with your hands on my hips
I want it to be a night we'll never forget
By showing you how I feel since the moment we met

Prince

I'm going through some things right now that I just can't
explain
Glad to know you're there to help me ease the pain
Your personality is soothing like the sound of dropping rain
Got to know more about you I just can't abstain
I'm glad we got to talking so let me open the champagne
And toast to the prince who just increased his reign
Poetically inspiring he shines like a platinum chain
His honesty and friendship I hope that I can gain

Toast to the Prince

He Made Me

I slowly crings and feel a wave of warmth over my body
Tiny creavasses are on my skin… he gave me goosebumps
Looking into his eyes a sensation that words cant describe
A smile peaks through.. He just made me blush
An overwhelming feeling of excitement when we meet
I no longer remain calm… He gave me butterflies
Positive thoughts of something he made me feel that's so real
The tears fill up my eyes… He just made me cry
Relaxation settles in because I know these feelings are mutual
Im no longer afraid of us… I think I just fell in love.

This is the latest to my collection. *"Little feet"* is dedicated to my son Jamil Angel Bautista. Since the day he was born he has shown to be a little trooper. He is curious, ambitious, full of life and has a Huge imagination for such a little person. My son is what keeps me going every day. I live for him and I am so glad to be his mom.

Little Feet

Little toes, little feet
He takes his first step, they're my little feet
Soft and small with little toe nails
just the perfect size to my surprise
those little feet start to fly
Gliding through the hard wood floor
one step at a time they start to sore
Not sure of where they will go next
It's a big world out there, just right ahead
Little toes, little feet
He takes his first steps, but they're no longer my little feet
My little boy has learned to walk,
not scared of life, not scared to fall.

Nueva Vida

No veo el momento en que tengas el bebe
Vas a estar sonriente eso si lo se
Los dos agarados de las manos
Tu bebe sonriendo con tus abrasos
Un mes y medio no puedes trabajar
Pero los dos juntos lo pueden pasar
Mama y bebe y una vida nueva
Te deseo lo mejor porque tu niño te espera

Matrimoñio

Siempre es bueno mantener un buen hogar

Pero nada es mas importante que un matrimono, eso es especial

Una vida nueva que van a empesar

Los dos juntos lo pueden pasar

Ahora que estan jovenes pueden disfrutar

Lo que la vida les traiga y lo tienen que gosar

Yo los quiero mucho a los dos

Aunque no los tengo a mi lado siempre recuerdo su vos

En este dia tan especial me gustaria decir

Que pase lo que pase, siempre estare aqui

Feliz Anniversario

Contigo, mi vida se a convertido en un sueño
De amor y alegria y todo lo bueno
Las cosas hermosas que hemos pasado,
Nuestro hogar, nuestro hijo, todo a tu lado
Por Buenos tiempos y por malos tiempos estamos casados
Siempre unidos y agarados de las manos
Te amo tanto que te quiero decir
Que gracias por estos 3 años que me diste por vivir
Hoy es nuestro anniversario y los que faltan por llegar
Te amo con todo mi Corazon y aqui siempre estara

About the Author

Janine Hernandez is a well renowned author, speaker, mentor, and world changer. She was awarded the 2011 Mitch Akin mentor of the Year Award (New Pathways Program). She holds a Masters of Arts in International Business from Western International University. Janine's sole purpose in life is to impact other woman and has partnered up with PGP and introduced a "Women's Empowerment Event". Janine is available for speaking engagements, keynote presentations, panel discussions, life/motivational coaching, corporate event planning, business consulting and book publishing.

Connect with Janine

Facebook.com/Janine.hernandez
Instagram.com/Janine.hdz5301
Instagram.com/purposedriveninitiatives
Linkedin Janine Hernandez
Purposedriveninitiatives@yahoo.com
www.PurposeDrivenInitiatives.com
www.pdi-publishing.com

Artist, Cristina Acosta is a painter, author and color expert.
See more of her work at www.CristinaAcosta.com

Front Cover Artwork:
The Dreamer and Her Angel, painted by Cristina Acosta
Acrylic and hard pastel with metal lead on 100% cotton rag
paper, 30"x 22".

In this image the Angel visits the Dreamer as she sleeps,
dusting her with stars and flowers. He represents her dream
and desire to be protected, nurtured and cherished. He is made
of golden starlight, high light color in contrast to her rich earth
color; he is the yang and she the yin, formed from the swirling
energy of the cosmos. He is a manifestation of the Dreamer
brought into reality from the flow of her thoughts. He is both
her animus and her dream lover. Dusted with the beauty of the
cosmos she will awaken fully to her consciousness.

PDI Publishing Official Sponsors and Partners

We Got Now Entertainment LLC
www.YNTSpeaks.com

Ian Designs LLC
Facebook.com/Iandesigns
Iandesigns.org

Live Entertainment LLC
jrockj2@hotmail.com

Pretty Girl Progression LLC
Instagram.com/PGProgression

Cristina Acosta Art & Design LLC
www.CristinaAcosta.com

Celeste S. Duckworth
Celesteduckworth@live.com

THE END